CONTENTS

PALAEOZOIC

541–252 MILLION YEARS AGO

Life Before Dinosaurs

Palaeozoic means 'old life' in Greek and describes the world before the dinosaurs. The land at this time forms one giant continent called Pangaea. It is populated with giant insects and strange animals called synapsids. The seas are filling up with early types of fish, too – but a big disaster is coming ...

Some familiar creatures inhabit the seas, including sharks, jellyfish and coral-like organisms.

This Helicoprion is an odd-looking 12-m-long shark with a set of teeth like a circular saw.

Trilobites have been swimming in the oceans for over 270 million years, but they will not survive much longer.

Jellyfish are very simple sea creatures that drift on the ocean currents, just like they do today. Very few jellyfish fossil records exist because they are 95 per cent water and have no bones.

At the end of the Palaeozoic period there is a mass extinction of plants and animals. Scientists today are not really sure why ...

Animals may have died after the impact of a large meteor crashing to Earth. Maybe it's down to global warming, or gases from volcanoes poisoning the air and water. Perhaps a lot of disasters happen at the same time.

Insects are huge because there is much more oxygen in the air. This dragonfly is the size of a seagull!

Nearly all of life on Earth is killed off, leaving just a few species … including your ancestors! Luckily for you they survived or you wouldn't be here!

Forests are made up of conifers, ferns, ginkgos, cycads and mosses. Lots of these plants die and fall into swamps. Over millions of years they turn into coal (a fossil fuel).

Some animals, like this Dimetrodon, fall into swamps when they die. Over the following billions of years they become fossilised. Eventually, the fossils are dug up and studied in museums.

5

MID-TRIASSIC
252–247 MILLION YEARS AGO

The Ancestors of the Dinosaurs

The dramatic extinction event at the end of the Palaeozoic period destroys up to 95 per cent of life on Earth. It is good news for those that survived though – such as the therapsids and the archosaurs – because they are able to adapt to the harsh new conditions that exist.

This plant-eating Asilisaurus is a type of archosaur. It is between 1 and 3 m long. Its name means 'ancestor lizard' because its descendants became the dinosaurs, crocodiles and birds.

· ASILISAURUS ·
LENGTH: 3 M
WEIGHT: 25 KG

The Coelophysis is another archosaur. It's a quick, two-legged predator that hunts for smaller lizards. Look, it has caught a small Euparkeria!

· LYSTROSAURUS ·
LENGTH: 1 M
WEIGHT: 90 KG

· COELOPHYSIS ·
LENGTH: 3 M
WEIGHT: 20 KG

· EUPARKERIA ·
LENGTH: 50 CM
WEIGHT: 5 KG

The Lystrosaurus is a type of therapsid. It's a distant ancestor of you and all other mammals. Its name means 'shovel lizard' because it uses massive forelimbs to dig burrows.

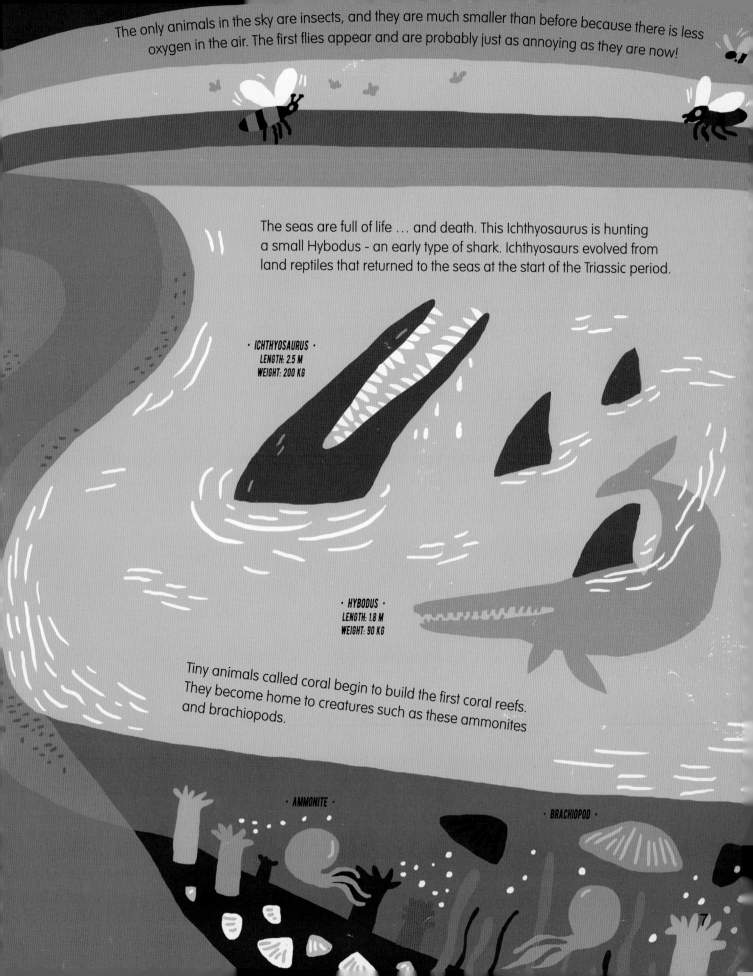

The only animals in the sky are insects, and they are much smaller than before because there is less oxygen in the air. The first flies appear and are probably just as annoying as they are now!

The seas are full of life ... and death. This Ichthyosaurus is hunting a small Hybodus - an early type of shark. Ichthyosaurs evolved from land reptiles that returned to the seas at the start of the Triassic period.

· ICHTHYOSAURUS ·
LENGTH: 2.5 M
WEIGHT: 200 KG

· HYBODUS ·
LENGTH: 1.8 M
WEIGHT: 90 KG

Tiny animals called coral begin to build the first coral reefs. They become home to creatures such as these ammonites and brachiopods.

· AMMONITE ·

· BRACHIOPOD ·

7

The Birth of the Dinosaurs

By the time of the Late Triassic period, life is recovering. The vast conifer forests are home to a growing range of animals. The seas are also filled with an increasing variety of life.

The Saltopus is quite small and has to be wary of threats from the skies, such as swooping pterosaurs. Saltopus is thought by many to be one of the first proper dinosaurs.

· SALTOPUS ELGINENSIS ·
LENGTH: 80-100 CM
WEIGHT: 1 KG

· PROGANOCHELYS QUENSTEDI ·
LENGTH: 1 M
WEIGHT: 36 KG

· CHINLECHELYS TENERTESTA ·
LENGTH: 30 CM
WEIGHT: 1.5 KG

Proganochelys and Chinlechelys are early types of turtle. They are hunting for fish. Proganochelys can use the small club on its tail to fight off Chinlechelys.

Shonisaurus looks on from the depths. When the fight above is over, this sea monster will try to gobble them all up!

· SHONISAURUS ·
LENGTH: 15 M
WEIGHT: 30,000 KG

The pterosaurs are the first animals with a backbone to fly. They swoop and soar, looking for fish or smaller lizards to snap up.

The Eoraptor is another early dinosaur. Its body is adapted for speed and agility to catch and eat smaller animals.

· EORAPTOR LUNENSIS ·
LENGTH: 1 M
WEIGHT: 10 KG

· HESPEROSUCHUS AGILIS ·
LENGTH: 1.5 M
WEIGHT: 36 KG

Although it is the size and shape of a greyhound dog, Hesperosuchus is actually an early form of crocodile.

· RIOJASAURUS ·
LENGTH: 10 M
WEIGHT: 1,000–3,000 KG

· MELANOROSAURUS ·
LENGTH: 8 M
WEIGHT: 1,100 KG

· MUSSAURUS ·
LENGTH: 3 M
WEIGHT: 70 KG

Riojasaurus, Mussaurus and Melanorosaurus are herbivorous dinosaurs. This means they are plant eaters.

9

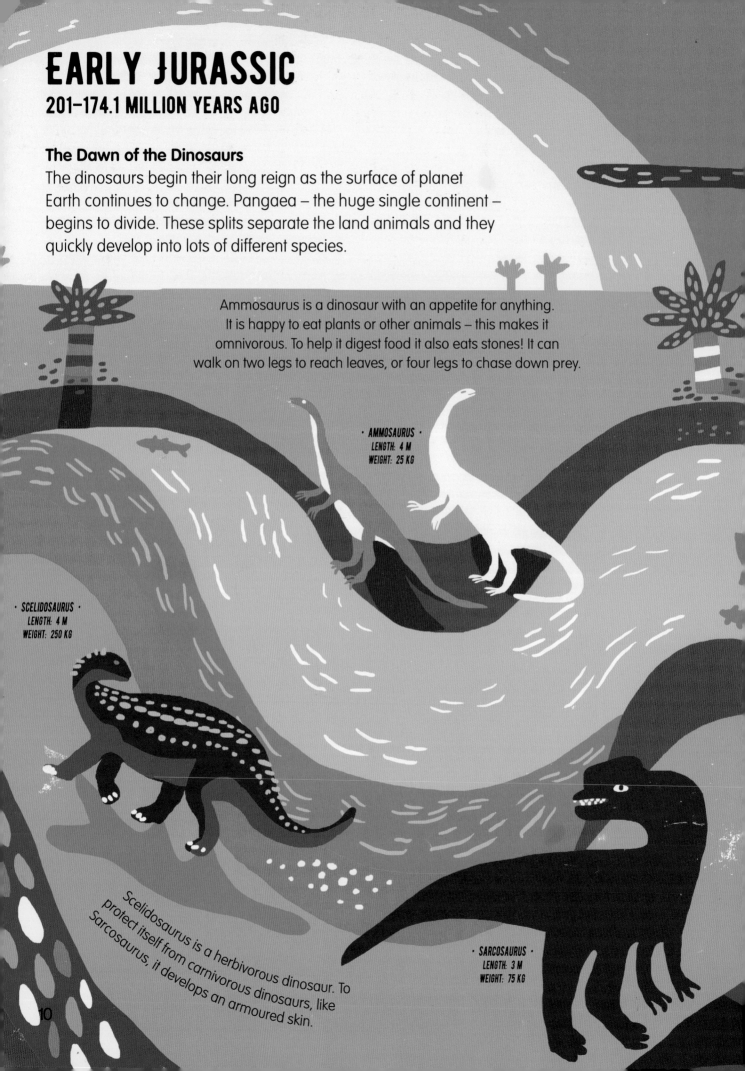

EARLY JURASSIC
201–174.1 MILLION YEARS AGO

The Dawn of the Dinosaurs

The dinosaurs begin their long reign as the surface of planet Earth continues to change. Pangaea – the huge single continent – begins to divide. These splits separate the land animals and they quickly develop into lots of different species.

Ammosaurus is a dinosaur with an appetite for anything. It is happy to eat plants or other animals – this makes it omnivorous. To help it digest food it also eats stones! It can walk on two legs to reach leaves, or four legs to chase down prey.

· AMMOSAURUS ·
LENGTH: 4 M
WEIGHT: 25 KG

· SCELIDOSAURUS ·
LENGTH: 4 M
WEIGHT: 250 KG

Scelidosaurus is a herbivorous dinosaur. To protect itself from carnivorous dinosaurs, like Sarcosaurus, it develops an armoured skin.

· SARCOSAURUS ·
LENGTH: 3 M
WEIGHT: 75 KG

The pterosaurs in the skies are also changing. Some are getting bigger, while others are developing crests on their heads. Some are even growing fur!

· DORYGNATHUS ·
WINGSPAN: 4.5 M
WEIGHT: 90 KG

· DIMORPHODON ·
WINGSPAN: 1.4 M
WEIGHT: 2 KG

Prosalirus is an early type of frog that lives and breeds in and around rivers. It eats insects and other small creatures.

· PLESIOSAURUS ·
LENGTH: 3.5 M
WEIGHT: 350 KG

Plesiosaurs, with their snake-like necks and barrel bodies, are common in this period. They rival the ichthyosaurs in size and they hunt for fish. Despite living in the sea, both these animals breathe air.

Heterodontosaurus means 'many-toothed' lizard. This small, omnivorous dinosaur has three different types of teeth and a beak!

· HETERODONTOSAURUS ·
LENGTH: 1.2 M
WEIGHT: 6 KG

MID-JURASSIC
174.1–163.5 MILLION YEARS AGO

The Rise of the Dinosaurs

As the Jurassic period progresses, the dinosaurs increase in number and body size. They lumber around forests filled with conifers, ferns, ginkgos, mosses and cycads, searching for food and trying to survive.

As the supercontinent of Pangaea continues to split, plates of land push together to create valleys and mountain ranges. In other places land pulls apart, creating ocean rifts.

The Megalosaurus is a type of theropod. This dinosaur is one of the most fearsome beasts around. Megalosaurus lives to hunt and kill, using its savage teeth and huge jaws to crush smaller creatures. Here one is stalking a Huayangosaurus.

· HUAYANGOSAURUS ·
LENGTH: 4.5 M
WEIGHT: 3,000 KG

· MEGALOSAURUS ·
LENGTH: 9 M
WEIGHT: 3,000 KG

The Huayangosaurus is a 4.5-m-long stegosaur (dinosaurs with plates along their spines). The plates and the spikes on its tail can be a useful defence.

Yinlong (meaning 'hidden dragon') likes to eat stones. The stones stay in its stomach and help to grind up the plants it eats.

· YINLONG ·
LENGTH: 1.2 M
WEIGHT: 15 KG

Sauropods have small heads on long necks, big bodies and long tails. They use their long necks to reach the leaves at the tops of trees.

This plant-eating Cetiosaurus is one of the early sauropods.

· CETIOSAURUS ·
LENGTH: 16 M
WEIGHT: 11,000 KG

· TIANCHISAURUS ·
LENGTH: 3 M
WEIGHT: 200 KG

· EUSTREPTOSPONDYLUS ·
LENGTH: 6 M
WEIGHT: 500 KG

Tianchisaurus is an armoured plant-eater – a type of ankylosaur. These dinosaurs are tough and have tail clubs. Ankylosaurs and stegosaurs belong to the ornithischian dinosaur group.

Eustreptospondylus is a theropod. Theropods usually eat meat and normally walk on two legs. They use their smaller front claws and arms to grip prey.

13

LATE JURASSIC
163.5–145 MILLION YEARS AGO

· ARCHAEOPTERYX ·
WINGSPAN: 50 CM
WEIGHT: 1 KG

The Land of the Dinosaurs
The Late Jurassic period sees the super continent Pangaea continuing to slowly tear itself in two, and there is a lot of volcanic activity.

The Archaeopteryx is a bird-like dinosaur of the theropod family, with wings and feathers. It is about the size of a raven, but unlike modern birds it has teeth.

As the period ends, the land masses split into the continents that we know today, although they still look very different. The turbulent land is now full of some of the most familiar dinosaurs.

The continents that are now North America, Europe and Asia are stuck together in Laurasia (in the north), while Gondwana (in the south) contains South America, Africa, India, Antarctica and Australia.

Stegosaurus, like all dinosaurs, lays eggs. Many dinosaurs made nests for their eggs – possibly to try to protect them from small theropods like Compsognathus.

· STEGOSAURUS ·
LENGTH: 9 M
WEIGHT: 3,000 KG

· COMPSOGNATHUS ·
LENGTH: 1.4 M
WEIGHT: 3 KG

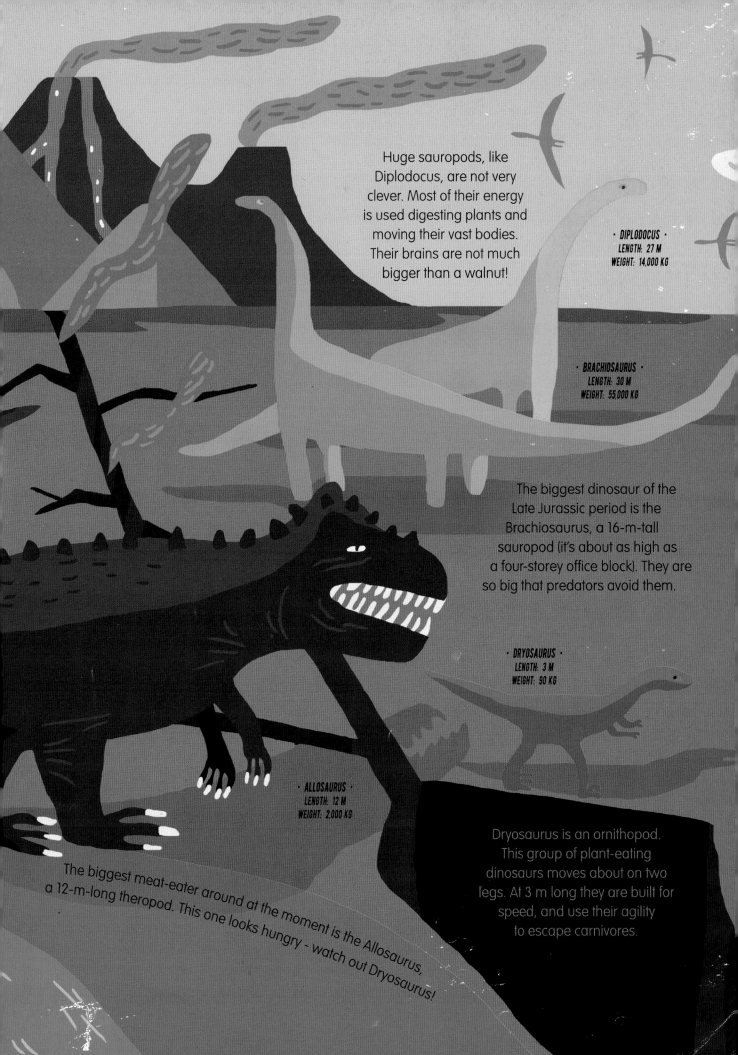

Huge sauropods, like Diplodocus, are not very clever. Most of their energy is used digesting plants and moving their vast bodies. Their brains are not much bigger than a walnut!

· DIPLODOCUS ·
LENGTH: 27 M
WEIGHT: 14,000 KG

· BRACHIOSAURUS ·
LENGTH: 30 M
WEIGHT: 55,000 KG

The biggest dinosaur of the Late Jurassic period is the Brachiosaurus, a 16-m-tall sauropod (it's about as high as a four-storey office block). They are so big that predators avoid them.

· DRYOSAURUS ·
LENGTH: 3 M
WEIGHT: 90 KG

· ALLOSAURUS ·
LENGTH: 12 M
WEIGHT: 2,000 KG

The biggest meat-eater around at the moment is the Allosaurus, a 12-m-long theropod. This one looks hungry - watch out Dryosaurus!

Dryosaurus is an ornithopod. This group of plant-eating dinosaurs moves about on two legs. At 3 m long they are built for speed, and use their agility to escape carnivores.

LATE JURASSIC
163.5–145 MILLION YEARS AGO

The Savage Seas

It isn't just on land that life is flourishing; the oceans are getting crowded, too. It is around this time that the Atlantic Ocean forms, as Pangaea splits into two supercontinents: Laurasia moves north, and Gondwana goes south. The waters are warm and filled with predators and their prey.

The fearsome Machimosaurus is a huge sea crocodile. Its long nose is designed to catch fish, but it also likes to snack on turtles, like this Pleurosternon.

· MACHIMOSAURUS ·
LENGTH: 9 M
WEIGHT: 2,500 KG

· PLEUROSTERNON ·
LENGTH: 2 M
WEIGHT: 30 KG

Coral reefs are getting bigger and offer a new habitat for all the different types of life that are evolving.

Under the seabed, billions of dead, microscopic creatures are being slowly crushed. Over millions of years they will turn into oil – the same oil we use to generate energy today.

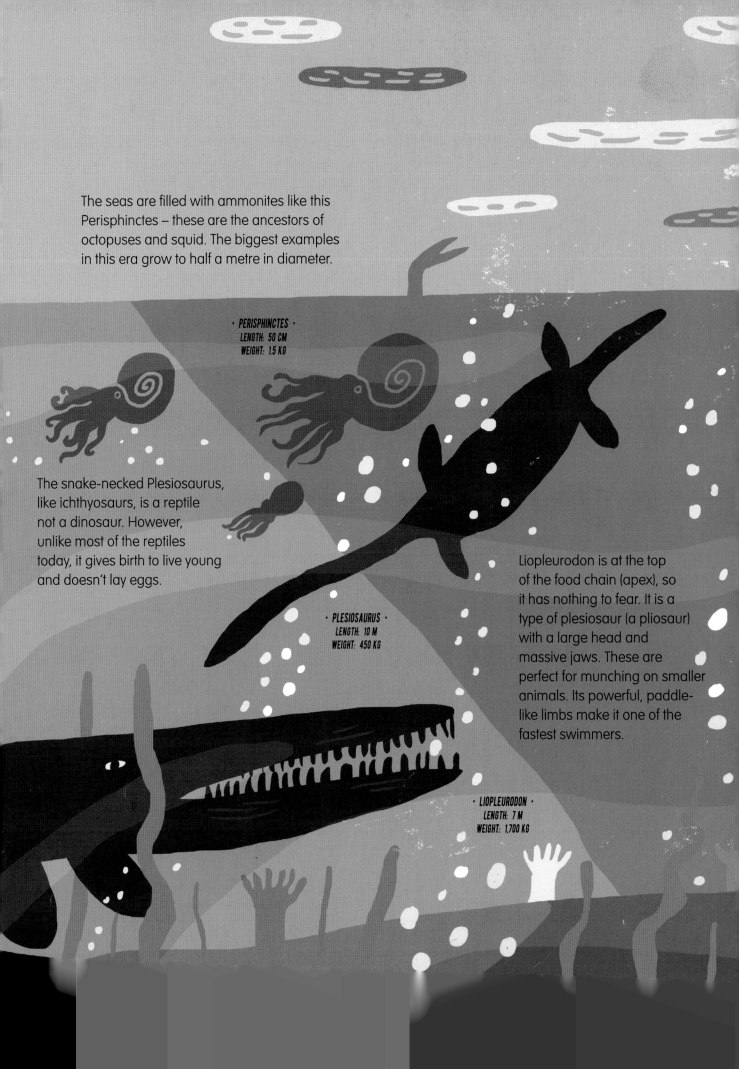

The seas are filled with ammonites like this Perisphinctes – these are the ancestors of octopuses and squid. The biggest examples in this era grow to half a metre in diameter.

· PERISPHINCTES ·
LENGTH: 50 CM
WEIGHT: 1.5 KG

The snake-necked Plesiosaurus, like ichthyosaurs, is a reptile not a dinosaur. However, unlike most of the reptiles today, it gives birth to live young and doesn't lay eggs.

· PLESIOSAURUS ·
LENGTH: 10 M
WEIGHT: 450 KG

Liopleurodon is at the top of the food chain (apex), so it has nothing to fear. It is a type of plesiosaur (a pliosaur) with a large head and massive jaws. These are perfect for munching on smaller animals. Its powerful, paddle-like limbs make it one of the fastest swimmers.

· LIOPLEURODON ·
LENGTH: 7 M
WEIGHT: 1,700 KG

EARLY CRETACEOUS
145–100.5 MILLION YEARS AGO

· VOLATICOTHERIUM ·
LENGTH: 30 CM
WEIGHT: 70 G

The Reign of the Dinosaurs

Dinosaurs are now at their biggest and most dominant, but other life is blooming too. The plant world has a new member – the angiosperm – that uses flowers to produce seeds. Insects are diversifying too, and so are the animals that eat them! The Volaticotherium is a mammal that glides from tree to tree catching bugs.

· DAKOSAURUS ·
LENGTH: 5 M
WEIGHT: 800 KG

The seas are ruled by reptile pliosaurs, such as Dakosaurus and Kronosaurus. If they can't find enough fish to eat they are likely to start lunching on each other!

· KRONOSAURUS ·
LENGTH: 9 M
WEIGHT: 7,000 KG

Archaeamphora is one of the earliest carnivorous plants – it traps and eats insects.

· ARCHAEAMPHORA ·
HEIGHT: 55 MM

With a magnificent fin on its back, it is easy to see how Spinosaurus got its name. It is a type of theropod and may be one of the biggest meat-eaters ever to walk the planet. It spends most of its time in the water and mainly eats fish, but will happily snap up a pterosaur if it gets the chance.

· SPINOSAURUS ·
LENGTH: 18 M
WEIGHT: 20,000 KG

· IGUANODON ·
LENGTH: 10 M
WEIGHT: 5,000 KG

In millions of years' time the Iguanodon will be one of the first dinosaurs to be found and named. For quite some time people will think that its spiky thumb is a horn on its head!

Psittacosaurus means 'parrot lizard' and it is a type of ceratopsian. Ceratopsians are plant-eating dinosaurs with beak-like mouths.

· PSITTACOSAURUS ·
LENGTH: 2 M
WEIGHT: 80 KG

Sinosauropteryx is a meat-eating dinosaur, about the size of a cat, that is covered in feathers. It may also have had reddish-brown stripes.

· SINOSAUROPTERYX ·
LENGTH: 1 M
WEIGHT: 500 G

A new type of insect has appeared — the wasp! The unlucky wasp is being attacked by a spider.

ŁATE CRETACEOUS

100.5–66 MILLION YEARS AGO

The Day of the Dinosaurs

The landscape is changing as plants evolve quickly. More flowers appear and many tree varieties grow, such as magnolias. The planet's continents look more like they do today, but are closer to each other. The planet is warmer than today, but is starting to cool, and the air is filled with lots of bird-like dinosaurs.

This Tyrannosaurus rex is probably the favourite to win this battle (just look at those metre-long jaws and its 23-cm-long teeth). The Triceratops has a chance though – if it can spear the T. rex with one of its mighty metre-long horns.

· TRICERATOPS ·
LENGTH: 9 M
WEIGHT: 26,000 KG

· TYRANNOSAURUS REX ·
LENGTH: 12 M
WEIGHT: 14,000 KG

· PINACOSAURUS ·
LENGTH: 5 M
WEIGHT: 1,900 KG

Pinacosaurus is a type of ankylosaur. Its massive club-like tail is perfect for defending attacks from other dinosaurs.

The biggest flying creature ever is the Quetzalcoatlus. On the ground it walks on all fours, searching for smaller animals to eat. In the air it uses its 11-m wingspan to soar through the sky.

· QUETZALCOATLUS ·
WINGSPAN: 11 M
WEIGHT: 120 KG

· GALLIMIMUS ·
LENGTH: 6 M
WEIGHT: 200 KG

Gallimimus is one of the fastest of the dinosaurs. It is similar in shape to a modern ostrich, and runs as fast – nearly 70 kph! It is omnivorous, eating plants and small animals.

Another speedy creature is the Velociraptor. It is small (about the size of a chicken) but extremely vicious. Here are some attacking a Protoceratops.

· MOSASAURUS ·
LENGTH: 15 M
WEIGHT: 14,000 KG

· VELOCIRAPTOR ·
LENGTH: 2 M
WEIGHT: 15 KG

The ruler of the seas is the Mosasaurus. This one is hunting a giant 5-m-wide turtle, called an Archelon.

· ARCHELON ·
LENGTH: 4 M
WEIGHT: 2,200 KG

· PROTOCERATOPS ·
LENGTH: 2 M
WEIGHT: 180 KG

LATE CRETACEOUS
100.5–66 MILLION YEARS AGO

The Night of the Dinosaurs
While the dinosaurs sleep, another type of animal comes out to play.
At this time, mammals are mostly nocturnal – meaning they are awake
at night time and asleep during the day. This habit has probably evolved
to avoid being around hungry dinosaurs!

· HESPERORNIS ·
LENGTH: 1.5 M
WEIGHT: 1 KG

The Hesperornis is a flightless marine bird. It lives
mostly at sea, but can sometimes be found in
freshwater rivers. It is agile in the water but moves
clumsily on land – a bit like a seal.

Tusoteuthis is a giant squid that can reach
up to 11 m in length. Despite its size it can
still be prey for other creatures. This one is
fighting with a ray-finned fish called a
Cimolichthys.

· TUSOTEUTHIS ·
LENGTH: 11 M
WEIGHT: 250 KG

· CIMOLICHTHYS ·
LENGTH: 2 M
WEIGHT: 35 KG

Most mammals of the period are more like Zalambdalestes, a 20-cm-long insect-eater. It hops on long back legs.

· ZALAMBDALESTES ·
LENGTH: 20 CM
WEIGHT: 3 G

· REPENOMAMUS ·
LENGTH: 1 M
WEIGHT: 5 KG

The largest of the mammals at this time is Repenomamus giganticus, and it is only 1 m long. Despite its small size it is capable of catching small dinosaurs like this young Psittacosaurus.

· (YOUNG) PSITTACOSAURUS ·
LENGTH: 2 M
WEIGHT: 20 KG

Ptilodus is about the size of a squirrel. It has a long tail and feet that can turn back on themselves. This makes Ptilodus well-suited to living in trees, where it probably eats a mixture of insects and plants.

· PTILODUS ·
LENGTH: 40 CM
WEIGHT: 6.5 G

Oxlestes is another large meat-eating mammal. This one is taking the easier option of digging up and eating dinosaur eggs.

· OXLESTES ·
LENGTH: 25 CM
WEIGHT: 4 KG

LATE CRETACEOUS
66 MILLION YEARS AGO

The Fall of The Dinosaurs

The reign of the dinosaurs came to an end about 66 million years ago. A 10-km-wide asteroid-like object struck the Earth near Mexico's Yucatan Peninsula. The impact created a 180-km-wide crater!

Soon after, 75 per cent of life on Earth was wiped out. Very few animals larger than a labrador dog survived ...

After the asteroid strikes, red-hot rock and debris is thrown into the air. The heat causes forest fires that create smoke and ash. This will stay in the air for months, preventing sunlight from reaching Earth. This kills off most of the plant life that is a vital food source.

· ARGENTINOSAURUS ·
LENGTH: 35 M
WEIGHT: 100,000 KG

The bodies of dinosaurs, such as this huge Argentinosaurus, will provide food for scavenging animals in the cold months to come.

When so many animals are killed
in such a short time, food chains
collapse. Even if dinosaurs, such as this
meat-eating Daspletosaurus, survive
the blast, they will starve because
there are too few animals to eat.

· DASPLETOSAURUS ·
LENGTH: 9 M
WEIGHT: 3,800 KG

Small omnivores and
carrion-eaters are best adapted
to survive. Omnivores, like these
Oviraptors, will eat anything: living
flesh, rotting dead bodies or plants.

· OVIRAPTOR ·
LENGTH: 1.5 M
WEIGHT: 30 KG

This coelurosaur is about to be hit
by a falling tree, and sap will cover its
body. Over millions of years this sap
will turn into amber and preserve it.

· COELUROSAUR ·
LENGTH: 2.5 M
WEIGHT: 25 KG

· NAJASH ·
LENGTH: 1.5 M
WEIGHT: 1 KG

· PURGATORIUS ·
LENGTH: 15 CM
WEIGHT: 3.5 G

Small creatures, like this two-legged snake-
like creature, Najash, and this early mammal,
Purgatorius, have the best chance of survival

THE TIMELINE UNDER OUR FEET

The mass extinction 66 million years ago was the end of many species. Those that survived continued to change – to evolve. One ape-like species evolved a brain that could use tools and develop language. It turned into us!

Not many animals that die become fossils. Usually they are eaten by scavengers or rot away, leaving no trace. The most common way for animals to become fossils is for them to die near water or mud.

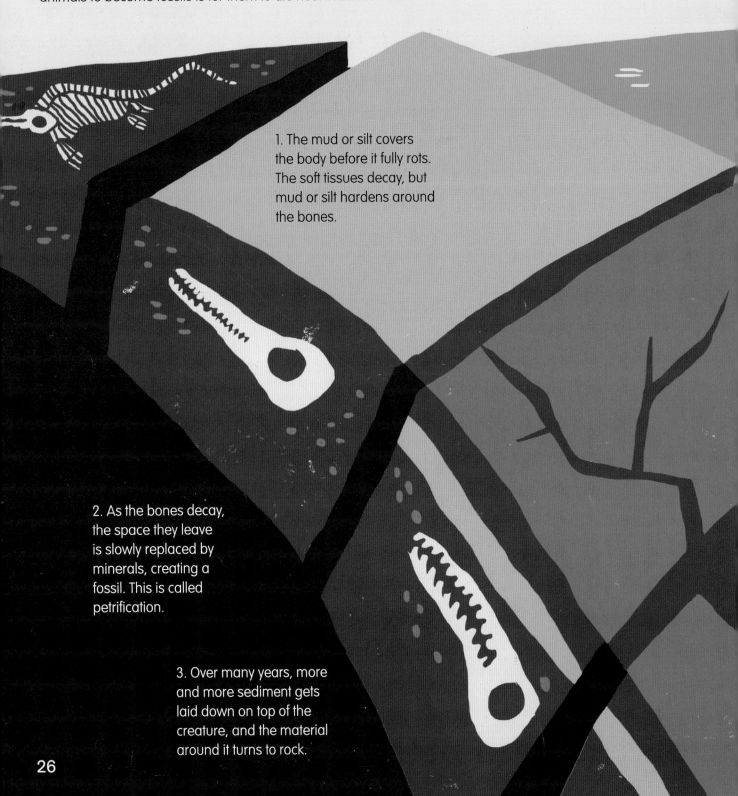

1. The mud or silt covers the body before it fully rots. The soft tissues decay, but mud or silt hardens around the bones.

2. As the bones decay, the space they leave is slowly replaced by minerals, creating a fossil. This is called petrification.

3. Over many years, more and more sediment gets laid down on top of the creature, and the material around it turns to rock.

People have found the remains of creatures in rocks for thousands of years. They thought they were dragons or ogres! It was only in the early 19th century that palaeontology – the study of history through fossils – really became established. Fossil hunters, such as Mary Anning (1799–1847), dug up the fossils and made a little money selling them to collectors.

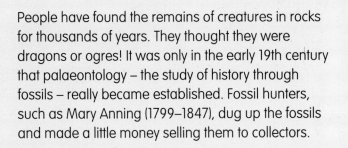

It wasn't all bad news for the dinosaurs. Most scientists are fairly certain that the small ones that survived the mass extinction event developed into birds.

Mary Anning reveals a fossilised ichthyosaur skeleton at the cliffs of Lyme Regis, UK, in 1811.

If you look at birds, like these seagulls, it's easy to imagine they are related to dinosaurs!

PALAEONTOLOGY TIMELINE

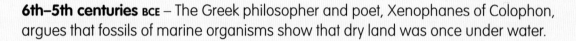

Over the last two centuries there have been many discoveries and different ideas about dinosaurs. Our knowledge of the past is limited to what we find, so every new discovery can change what we understand about prehistoric times quite a lot. Perhaps something completely new has been discovered since this book was written!

6th–5th centuries BCE – The Greek philosopher and poet, Xenophanes of Colophon, argues that fossils of marine organisms show that dry land was once under water.

1770s – The fossilised bones of a huge animal are found in a quarry near Maastricht in the Netherlands.

1801 – Naturalist Georges Cuvier writes that a drawing of a fossil found in Bavaria shows a flying reptile: in 1809 he names it Pterodactyl.

1808 – Georges Cuvier identifies an extinct marine reptile, and in 1822 William Conybeare names it Mosasaur.

1811 – Mary Anning and her brother Joseph discover the fossilised remains of an ichthyosaur at Lyme Regis, England.

1822 – Mary Mantell discovers some fossil teeth and her husband, Gideon, suggests they belong to an ancient reptile, which he names Ignuanodon.

1822 – Frenchman, Henri de Blanville, invents the word 'palaeontologie' to name the study of ancient animals and plants from fossils.

1823 – Mary Anning discovers the world's first plesiosaur skeleton at Lyme Regis, England.

1824 – William Buckland, working at Oxford University, names a fossil jaw Megalosaurus.

1829 – Buckland publishes a paper on the work he and Mary Anning had done identifying and analysing fossilised poo found at Lyme Regis and elsewhere. Buckland coins the term 'coprolite' for them, and uses them to analyse ancient food chains.

1831 – Mantell publishes an influential paper entitled 'The Age of Reptiles' summarising evidence of an extended period during which large reptiles had been the dominant animals.

1832 – Mantell puts together part of the skeleton of a Hylaeosaurus.

1836 – Edward Hitchcock describes the footprints of giant prehistoric birds found in rocks in Connecticut Valley, Massachusetts, USA.

1841 – John Phillips suggests that Earth's past history can be divided into three great periods of time: the Palaeozoic, Mesozoic and Cenozoic. He used fossil evidence in rocks to come up with this first geologic time scale.

1842 – Richard Owen, an anatomist and palaeontologist, recognises that Iguanodon, Megalosaurus and Hylaeosaurus all belonged to an ancient group of reptiles which he named Dinosauria.

1858 – Joseph Leidy identifies fossils excavated by William Foulke as the first dinosaur skeleton discovered in the USA.

1861 – The first Archaeopteryx skeleton is found in Bavaria, Germany, and recognised as a transitional form between reptiles and birds.

1871 – Othniel Charles Marsh discovers the first American pterosaur fossils.

1877 – The first Diplodocus fossil skeleton was found near Canon City, Colorado, USA and was named by Othniel Marsh in 1878.

1905 – Tyrannosaurus rex is described and named by Henry Fairfield Osborn.

1912 – Alfred Wegener proposes the theory of continental drift – that Earth's continents were once joined together but slowly moved apart over millions of years, offering an explanation for why similar fossils turn up on continents far apart from each other.

1912 – Eric Stromer, a German palaeontologist, discovers a skeleton of a large spiny dinosaur in Egypt and later names it Spinosaurus.

1980 – Luis Alvarez, Walter Alvarez, Frank Asaro and Helen Michel propose the Alvarez hypothesis: that a comet or asteroid struck the Earth 66 million years ago causing the Cretaceous–Paleogene extinction event, including the extinction of the non-avian dinosaurs.

1996 – Li Yumin, a Chinese farmer, discovers a dinosaur-like fossil with feathers and wings, later named Sinosauropteryx.

2004 – In Canada, scientists Ted Daeschler, Neil Shubin and Farish Jenkins discover fossils of a Tiktaalik, a fish with well-developed legs. It provides an evolutionary link between fish and land animals.

2010 – Palaeontologist Robert Bakker and his team excavate an almost complete Dimetrodon in Texas, USA.

2016 – Chinese palaeontologist, Lida Xing, discovers a fossil of a 99-million-year-old dinosaur preserved in amber in a market in Myanmar.

GLOSSARY

Ancestor: A plant, animal or living organism that is related or descended from a similar one from the past.

Ankylosaurus: A large four-legged, tank-like dinosaur covered in armour.

Archosaurs: The direct ancestors of the dinosaurs and modern animals such as birds and alligators.

Asteroid: A rock that orbits our Sun in space. These rocky objects are too small to be called planets but if a large asteroid hits Earth it could be catastrophic.

Carnivore: An animal that feeds on meat.

Carrion: The rotting flesh of dead animals.

Continent: The Earth currently has seven large land masses, each known as a continent. The continents are Europe, Asia, Africa, North America, South America, Australasia and Antarctica.

Coral: A tiny sea creature that can combine with millions of others to create a large stone structure out of its exoskeleton called a coral reef.

Cretaceous: The period of the Earth's history from 145.5–65.5 million years ago.

Cycad: An evergreen plant that looks like a cross between a fern and a palm.

Descendants: A person, plant, animal or living organism that is descended from (or related) to another of the same species from the past.

Dinosaurs: A group of land-living reptiles that were the most important land animals of the Triassic, Jurassic and Cretaceous periods.

Evolve: To change from one form to another over time and over many generations.

Extinction event: The extinction of a large number of species within a short space of time. This happens because of changes to the environment or a catastrophic global event like an asteroid strike.

Fern: A flowerless plant with feather-like fronds instead of leaves.

Forelimbs: Front legs.

Fossil: The remains of a prehistoric animal or plant that has been turned to stone and preserved for millions of years.

Ginkgo: A large tree with fan-shaped leaves that was abundant during the Jurassic period.

Global warming: The rising temperature of planet Earth is called global warming or climate change. As temperatures rise, glaciers melt and sea levels rise.

Jurassic: The period of Earth's history from 199.6–145.5 million years ago.

Mammal: An animal that gives birth to live young and feeds them on its own milk.

Meteor: A lump of rock floating in space that can sometimes fall through the atmosphere and crash into the Earth.

Moss: A plant with no flowers or roots.

Omnivore: An animal that eats both plants and animals.

Organism: Any individual living thing, such as an animal, plant or single-celled life form.

Ornithopod: A two-legged, plant-eating dinosaur.

Oxygen: A colourless and odourless gas that forms a large part of the air on Earth. Animals and plants need to breathe oxygen to live.

Pangaea: A supercontinent that existed from about 335 million years ago and split to form the modern-day continents.

Period: A division of time distinguished by the kinds of animals and plants that lived then. A period usually lasts for tens of millions of years.

Predator: An animal that hunts other animals for food.

Prehistoric: Before written history.

Prey: An animal that is hunted for food.

Pterosaur: A kind of flying reptile from the age of the dinosaurs.

Sauropod: Massive plant-eating dinosaurs with long necks and long tails.

Scavenging: Searching for anything to eat, usually from the remains of other creature's food.

Sediment: Mineral or organic matter deposited by water, air or ice.

Silt: Small particles of earth that are carried and then left behind by water.

Species: A group of animals or plants that have the same appearance as one another and can breed with one another.

Synapsids: A group of lizard-like animals that are the ancestors of mammals.

Therapsid: A mammal-like type of synapsid.

Theropod: A group of dinosaurs that includes all the meat-eaters.

Triassic Period: The period of Earth's history from 251–199.6 million years ago.

Trilobite: An extinct sea creature that is one of the earliest arthropods – a group that includes crabs, spiders and scorpions.

Wingspan: The size of a winged animal, measured from wingtip to wingtip when the wings are open.

FURTHER INFORMATION

Further Reading

34.7 Quadrillion Minutes Since the Last Dinosaurs Died (The Big Countdown series)
by Paul Mason (Franklin Watts)

Dinosaur Infosaurus series by Katie Woolley (Wayland)

Planet Earth: Birth of the Dinosaurs by Michael Bright (Wayland)

Darwin's Tree of Life by Michael Bright (Wayland)

Websites

www.natgeokids.com/uk/discover/animals/prehistoric-animals/steve_brusatte/

Keep up to date with new discoveries about dinosaurs on the National Geographic
Kids website. While you're there, read an interview with real-life palaeontologist and
dinosaur expert Steve Brusatte.

www.bbc.co.uk/programmes/b00sy534/clips

The BBC is the place to go for short videos about dinosaurs.

www.nhm.ac.uk/discover/dino-directory.html

All the facts and figures, plus extensive directories of all known prehistoric creatures
are at your fingertips at the website for the Natural History Museum in the UK.

www.amnh.org/dinosaurs

The American Museum of Natural History has a simple
and informative website for fans of dinosaurs. Check
out the videos, recorded by experts at the museum,
which provide fascinating facts and information
about dinosaurs.

**www.activewild.com/dinosaur-facts-
for-kids-students-and-adults/**

This wildlife and science website is packed with
dinosaur facts and figures. Have a specific question
about dinosaurs? Then the chances are you'll find the
answer here.

INDEX

Franklin Watts
Published in paperback in Great Britain in 2020 by
The Watts Publishing Group
Copyright © The Watts Publishing Group 2019
All rights reserved

Illustrator: Øivind Hovland
Design manager: Peter Scoulding
Executive editor: Adrian Cole
ISBN 978 1 4451 5856 3
Printed in China

Franklin Watts
An imprint of Hachette Children's Group
Part of The Watts Publishing Group
Carmelite House
50 Victoria Embankment
London EC4Y 0DZ
An Hachette UK Company
www.hachette.co.uk
www.franklinwatts.co.uk

MIX
Paper from responsible sources
FSC® C104740
www.fsc.org